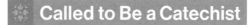
Called to Be a Catechist

FOSTERING
SPIRITUALITY

Inspiration and Professional Growth

TWENTY-THIRD
PUBLICATIONS
twentythirdpublications.com

IMPRIMATUR

✝ Most Reverend
  Robert J. McManus, STD,
  Bishop of Worcester,
  October 30, 2017

TWENTY-THIRD PUBLICATIONS
1 Montauk Avenue, Suite 200, New London, CT 06320
(860) 437-3012 » (800) 321-0411 » www.twentythirdpublications.com

Cover photo: ©iStockphoto.com / yelo34

ISBN: 978-1-62785-290-6
Library of Congress Catalog Card Number: 2017941590
Printed in the U.S.A.

 A division of Bayard, Inc.

CONTENTS

INTRODUCTION

We live in unsettling times. Our nation has been at war for more than a decade. The economy is shaky. Unemployment is a reality for many. The cost of higher education makes a college degree seem beyond reach. We are constantly bombarded with texts, e-mails, tweets, and information from technology that was supposed to make our lives less hectic. Kids doubt that the future holds the same promise and opportunities for them that it held for their parents.

Is it any wonder we long for a way to make sense of it all?

This book on spirituality speaks to our inner longing for deeper meaning in life and our quest for the holy. It will help you reflect on the meaning of spirituality; it challenges you to become a more spiritual person.

At each chapter's end, there are practical suggestions for adapting the ideas in the chapter to your ministry as a catechist. As you read (or re-read) the seven chapters, look for ways you can integrate the content into your lesson plans.

SPIRITUALITY *and* RELIGION: CHALLENGES *and* OPPORTUNITIES

FR. JAMES HEFT, SM

Influences like the internet, social media, television, and music can so powerfully impact one's identity that a person can lose touch with the religious traditions in which he or she has been raised.

I n the past few years, media coverage about the Catholic Church has not always inspired confidence. We continue to read about sexual abuse by our clergy, the large number of Catholics who have left the church for another faith or none at all (one in ten, according to a Pew Charitable Trust Survey), and the growing number of "nones," which is the increasing number of young Americans who no longer identify with any church or religion.

From 1970 to 1990, the number of people who identified themselves as "nones" stayed at about 7%. Starting in 1990, however, that number began to rise sharply, reaching 17% in 2010. And for those who are 18 to 29 years of age, that number rose steadily from 12% to 27%.

Couple these developments with another phenomenon—the increasing interest in "spirituality"—and we discover that the world we live in is complex, to say the least. A decline in religion and a growth in spirituality? Sociologists use the word *churn* to describe the current religious scene in the United States.

Religion: Changing and Surviving

These developments affect not only Christians, who constitute 85% of the United States. They also affect Jews and other religious people in the developed world. Jonathan Sacks, the Chief Rabbi of London from 1991-2013, asked why we need religion today to explain the universe since we have science, or to control the universe since we have technology. If we are ill, he continues, we go to a doctor, not a priest or a rabbi. If we feel guilty, we go to a psychiatrist, not to confession. Finally, he writes, "if you seek salvation you go to our new cathedrals, namely shopping centers, where you can buy happiness at extremely competitive prices" ("The Meaning-Seeking Animal," in *The Tablet*, November 14, 2009, p. 12).

Despite all this, religion has somehow survived. But it has changed as it has survived. What should we make of all this churning? What contributes to this new situation? What should we think of the so-called "spiritual but not religious" movement? Is it mainly a negative trend, a positive one, or both? And what approaches should religious educators and catechists take in the face of these developments?

Historical Background: It Isn't That New

I think it would help to understand that all this churning did not begin in the last decade or even in the fabled 1960s. Seeds sown by the European Enlightenment (think seventeenth and eighteenth centuries) began to take root and sprout practices in the eighteenth and nineteenth centuries that made religion (in this instance, Christianity) a private matter, best kept out of government and economic life. Mostly understood as only a family matter—a good way to raise children—religion, in the minds of these thinkers, became dangerous (even caused wars) when it reached into the public sphere with its dogmas and condemnations. By contrast, science is based on reason; these thinkers believed it was the sure path to a better future.

By the middle of the nineteenth century in the United States, influential writers like Ralph Waldo Emerson mocked organized religion (especially Calvinism) as rigid and irrelevant, and described preachers as bores.

At the beginning of the twentieth century, William James, a leading thinker in psychology and philosophy, described religion as "the feelings, acts and experiences of individual men in their solitude" (*The Varieties of Religious Experience*, Harmondsworth, Middlesex, England: Penguin, 1982, p. 31). He further explained that when people thought of religion, they thought of some church that suggested to them "so much hypocrisy and tyranny and meanness and tenacity of superstition" that they just dismissed it (p. 335). James wasn't especially happy about all this, but he did think religion was really best understood as what people experienced when they were alone and enjoyed deep thoughts. Today, in our urban environments, it's harder to be alone, and a dizzying array of media makes deep thoughts rare.

In the 1950s and 1960s, sociologists wrote about "teenagers" and "adolescents" as a stage brought about as a result of mass education, the legal condemnation of child labor, urbanization and suburbanization, and the creation of a consumer and entertainment culture. Now, instead of writing about the three stages of childhood, adolescence, and adulthood, sociologists have discovered that they have to insert a fourth stage: emerging adulthood.

Youth today physically mature sooner than before and assume adult responsibilities later than ever. One sociologist, Jeffrey Arnett, describes emerging adults as unstable, locked into prolonged identity searches, focused on themselves, feeling in limbo and transition, and, paradoxically, retaining a sense of possibility and hope. In a highly mobile society where the internet, social media, music, television, and movies can exert

> Today, in our urban environments, it's harder to be alone, and a dizzying array of media makes deep thoughts rare.

more powerful influence than a religious tradition or a single family, is it any wonder that an increasing number of emerging adults lose touch with the religious traditions in which they may have been raised?

Spiritual but Not Religious: Challenges

Christian Smith, an important sociologist of religion, describes the religious outlook of most U.S. teenagers as moral therapeutic deism (MTD). For them, religion has more to do with rules (morals) than relationships, gives great value to feeling good (therapeutic) about themselves, and speaks of God (deism) rather than of Jesus. They rarely spend time reading Scripture, and they don't understand the sacraments as encounters with Jesus. They are, as Smith describes them, "sub-trinitarian" (deism). Their lives are busy with school, social events, friends, texting, and entertainment; few of them give their religious faith top billing.

When teenagers get to college, they likely hear even more that being spiritual but not religious is to be more open, more adult, freer of the confining traditions of their parents, especially if their parents are religious. They might study a variety of religions and be taught that all religions are basically the same—teach the same values—and that what is most important is to be a good person. Many are taught that mature people transcend any one religious tradition and adopt a spirituality that embraces everyone.

Michael Lerner, a Jewish writer in the Reform tradition, described spirituality as "a feeling of awe, wonder, and radical amazement in response to the universe," an attitude that recognizes the "ultimate Unity of All Being" and the "sanctity" of every person. He continues: Spirituality is a trust that there is enough for everyone, and that the world is "filled with a conscious energy that transcends the categories and concepts" that religious people use to describe reality. By contrast, he describes religions as "various historical attempts to organize a set of doctrines, rituals, and specific practices which are supposed to be 'the right way to live'" ("Why Spirituality?" *Tikkum*, Vol. 15, No. 2, March/April 2000, pp. 7-8).

For people who root their spirituality in their religious tradition, such a sharp contrast between the two makes no sense. Opposing spirituality to religion often ends up in seeking spiritual highs without the discipline offered by a community and a tradition. Lawrence Cunningham, a keen Catholic observer of the spiritual life, warns that much of the spirituality market today is scarred by a highly narcissistic preoccupation not unlike old self-improvement schemes.

Spirituality and the Lived Experience

That said, it would be wise not to dismiss completely the hunger for spirituality as always narcissistic or a hobby of the self-absorbed. In the latter part of the twentieth century, major Catholic theologians who sometimes disagreed with each other nonetheless agreed that greater attention needed to be paid to the lived experience of people.

German theologian Karl Rahner believed that in our own time, if Christianity was to survive, it would have to become mystical. By mystical he was not suggesting that everyone had to have extraordinary religious experiences, such as visions or ecstasies. What he wanted to stress was that religious practices, to be authentic, needed to take root in daily living and the awareness of mystery—another easily misunderstood word that he simply used to refer to that deeper part of life that is not easily understood.

Similarly, Swiss theologian Hans Urs von Balthasar, who often sharply criticized Rahner, thought the perception of beauty—not only in art but in the lives of the saints, especially Christ, and indeed the crucified Christ—is what first attracts a person to living the Christian life. The Christian, von Balthasar was fond of saying, is in love with the love that appeared in Christ. Once this beauty and love are experienced, there is a desire to live the lives of beauty that they see in the saints, in the great works of art, in the glory of nature and of God's goodness. For him, truth should never be separated from love, which is the core of everything.

To mention just one more theological giant, Canadian theologian Bernard Lonergan, toward the end of his life, came to a similar conclusion: At the core of the Christian life is the experience of falling in love—the ultimate goal of life, where faith deepens by recognizing God's love for everyone.

All three of these highly influential theologians realized this: that the traditional objective proofs for God's existence, that an intellectual grasp of Catholic teachings, and that just keeping the rules—none of these by itself—makes people spiritually mature. In short, for all of them, love prepares the way for genuine faith.

> Many of our young people have been baptized but have not yet converted, have been catechized but have not yet fallen in love.

Taking these three theologians seriously suggests that the "spiritual but not religious" movement might actually be a positive development. Many of our young people have been baptized but have not yet converted, have been catechized but have not yet fallen in love. On the other hand, there are real risks, especially for those who no longer participate in the life of the church. The larger culture—primarily consumerist, materialist, and relativist—will offer them little encouragement to search deeply in their hearts for the meaning of life.

Suggestions for Religious Educators: Opportunities

It is important to remember that the Holy Spirit never abandons the church, and especially those who, with courage, competence, and generosity, try to pass on the tradition to the next generation. There should be little doubt that over the past sixty years or so, we have undergone a cultural, and therefore religious, revolution.

In the face of these massive shifts, what might be some fruitful approaches for religious educators, especially those who work with young people? I suggest five approaches. There are surely many others, but I have seen these bear real fruit among teenagers and young adults.

1. Intergenerational contact: Informed commentators on religious education stress the importance of family involvement. When parents don't support the religious education of their children, it is more difficult to make what children learn stay with them. Teachers need to get more adults, especially parents (they have more influence than they realize), involved in this effort.

2. *Service as an introduction to love:* The three famous theologians I mentioned earlier stressed the centrality of love as key to religious maturity. Young people who are encouraged to serve and help others acquire a "feel" for love. To link that love to the gospel and to the church is one of the privileges and tasks of religious educators.

3. *Silence for depth:* I am not against social media, the internet, or smart phones. I am against letting them dominate and distract us from a thoughtful existence. There is an appointed time for everything (Ecclesiastes), and one of those things is silence. Youth especially need to learn this discipline, and religious educators should have the courage to lead them into it.

4. *Community, a key context:* Christianity is like the common cold: it is contagious. You get it from those who have it. The Christian community includes more than one's contemporaries or one's fellow citizens. It reaches back in history and includes believers around the world. Telling our stories and listening to the stories of others helps ground us in a larger context and longer history.

5. *Doctrines, explanations, and reading:* Even though experience and especially love are key doorways into a deeper and more authentic religious life, words and explanations are very important. After all, Christianity is a religion of the Word, who not only demonstrated in his life and death what love is but also taught it. We need to be prepared to give an explanation for the hope that is within us (1 Peter 3:15). Increasing one's intellectual grasp of the faith actually deepens one's experience of it and equips a person to speak about it.

Love unexpressed in word and deed is not love. Acting on these five suggestions should help believers be both spiritual and religious.

9

Your Thoughts

1 What do I think are the qualities of a spiritually mature Catholic Christian?

_____

_____

2 What significant and recent experiences in my life have deepened my appreciation for the relationship of spirituality and religion?

_____

_____

_____

Try This

Make a list of all the religious traditions that are important to you. Consider how each one affects your identity as a Catholic. Then reflect on one religious tradition you would like to begin (for example, reading the Scriptures every day or joining a prayer group). Write a three-step action plan for incorporating this new practice into your life on a regular basis.

SCHOOLS *of* SPIRITUALITY

WILLIAM H. JOHNSTON

This chapter introduces four significant schools of spirituality: Benedictine, Dominican, Ignatian, and Eastern Catholic spirituality. Each offers a unique approach to prayer.

How do we discover the ways of prayer? We can learn at home from parents, at the parish from the liturgy or the parish staff, at school from teachers, under the guidance of a spiritual director, on our own from study, or simply by listening to the movements of our hearts as they turn to God in love. We can also learn from the riches of the church's tradition of prayer. From among many others, here are four sources from that tradition.

Benedictine

St. Benedict (sixth century) is a leading figure in the history of monasticism and the founder of the Benedictine family of religious communities. A brief phrase that expresses the charism of monastic life is *ora et labora*, "pray and work." This calls one to be devoted to God and to attend to the needs of self, community, and the wider world—a good recipe for a balanced life. At the heart of one's daily rhythm of prayer is Scripture, in particular the psalms—and this goes not only for Benedictines but for the whole church in its daily prayer of the Liturgy of the Hours.

A method of praying with Scripture that developed in the monastic tradition is known as *lectio divina*, a phrase often translated as "sacred reading." The method is ancient but remains fully relevant for us today.

Indeed, Pope Benedict XVI called for renewed attention to *lectio divina*, saying that he was convinced it could bring the church "a new spiritual springtime." Its four parts can be practiced in various ways. The approach presented here is very simple. While useful for anyone, it is especially helpful for those new to *lectio divina*.

What follows is based on "A Monastic Primer," found at the New Melleray Abbey website (newmelleray.org/primer.asp), where it is explained more fully and very beautifully.

The first step is reading (*lectio*). Beginning in a spirit of prayer, open your Bible to the passage you have selected and simply start to read. Read slowly. You are not in a hurry because your point is not to finish the reading but to let God speak to you, here and now, in and through the sacred text.

Then comes meditation (*meditatio*), sometimes referred to as repetition (*repetitio*). When a word or phrase grabs your attention and "speaks" to you, stop reading and simply stay with those words, prayerfully and slowly repeating them several times. No need to think about the text or draw lessons from it; just let God's inspired word do its healing, transforming work in you. Repeat the words in this slow, prayerful way for as long as they hold spiritual power. When that passes, continue reading.

During this process, you sometimes will be drawn to offer God a brief word of prayer. This is the third component (*oratio*). Perhaps the phrase you are meditating on leads you to say to God, in some way, "Thank you for..." or "I'm sorry that..." or "Please help me to...." Such prayers may be very brief; then return to the reading or meditation.

At times, this process may lead to an inner silence. Here, no words are used and no thoughts are thought. You simply are present with the Lord in a wordless, loving communication. This is a form of "contemplation" (*contemplatio*), a fourth aspect of *lectio divina*. Stay with this prayer as long as it lasts. When it ends, return again to the reading or meditation.

The regular practice of sacred reading will fill your mind and heart with a treasure trove of scriptural passages that can nourish your spirit with the power of God's word. This is an especially fitting method of prayer for catechists who serve as ministers of God's word.

Dominican

St. Dominic (thirteenth century) devoted his life to preaching the gospel. To be prepared for this ministry, Dominic and his followers devoted themselves to study. Of the various features of Dominican spirituality that we might highlight, let us focus here on this Dominican commitment to study, which they practice not as something alongside and separate from their prayer and spirituality but as a form of it. There is a true "spirituality of study" that all can cultivate—not only in preaching but in all forms of teaching and catechesis.

Anyone who teaches would want to learn more about those they teach (the learner), how to teach (the process of learning), and what they teach (their subject matter). A way to "pray" our studying of any of these topics is to begin and conclude times of study with moments of prayer, for ourselves that we may gain insight and wisdom, and for our students that they may benefit thereby.

But beyond this, the very act of studying and exercising the intellect God gave us in service to the welfare of others can become prayer. This happens when the time spent in study is also infused by the sheer joy of learning, and by our love—of the students we teach, of the subject we teach, of the knowledge and truth we seek to hand on, and of the Truth to whom we seek to lead our students, namely, Christ himself (John 14:6).

The more catechists can devote time to study in a spirit of prayer, the more their own catechist spirituality will be deepened and renewed.

> The more catechists can devote time to study in a spirit of prayer, the more their own catechist spirituality will be deepened and renewed.

Ignatian

St. Ignatius Loyola (sixteenth century), founder of the Society of Jesus, or Jesuits, was a master of the spiritual life because he reflected deeply on the ways he experienced God's love for him and learned how to discern God's presence and movement in his life. He became uniquely gifted in being able to guide and help others who sought to know God's love and hear God's call in their lives. The thirty-day retreat is perhaps the most famous way the Ignatian practice of discernment is carried on in the church today.

For those unable to take a month for such a retreat, there are other options. One is called the Nineteenth Annotation, where one does the retreat at home over the course of nine months or so, devoting an hour and a half each day to prayer and meeting with a retreat director weekly.

There is also an eight-day format that provides an abbreviated experience of the thirty-day retreat; for many, this opportunity can prove to be a time of rich blessings and even a turning point in their relationship with God. Even a weekend of prayer at a Jesuit retreat house provides a nourishing taste of what these longer retreats offer.

An Ignatian practice that anyone can use, and that St. Ignatius recommended highly, is the daily *examen*. It takes about fifteen minutes (less if need be), typically at the end of the day. The basic steps are these.

First, let yourself be still and come to rest in the presence of God. Then recall God's many good gifts to you, especially those of this particular day, and be thankful.

Second, pray that God enlighten your vision and memory to give you a Holy-Spirit-guided perspective on your life, and then ask yourself two questions.

- *How was God present and active in my life today?* Some people review their day like they were watching a movie, while others just let moments arise to consciousness as they will. Either method works. As you recall what happened, ask yourself:

14

- *How did I respond to God's presence today?* See what moments in the day draw your attention. Be honest—and talk with God about how things went. In a way, this is the heart of the daily examen. What do you learn in this conversation with God?

Third, for the times you may have neglected God's call, were slow to respond, or were sinful, ask for God's merciful forgiveness and for healing and strength to be able to respond in a more faithful and loving way in the future. Then look forward to tomorrow, asking for God's presence and guidance in a spirit of hope and trust.

Careful and prayerful meditation of this kind each day will help one become more attuned to God's movement and faithful to God's call in life.

> St. John Paul II often said that the church would be healthier if we breathed from both lungs— that is, from the Christian traditions of East and West.

Eastern Catholic Spirituality

St. John Paul II often said that the church would be healthier if we breathed from both lungs—that is, from the Christian traditions of East and West. If we took his advice, those of the Western tradition (such as Roman Catholics) would try to learn something from those of the Eastern tradition. Doing so might lead us to a deeper value of silence, the beauty of the liturgy, or praying with icons.

Here let me recommend a form of prayer more commonly practiced in the Christian East, often known as the Jesus Prayer. I first learned of this prayer in my college days by reading R. M. French, *The Way of a Pilgrim* (Carol Stream, IL: Hope Publishing House, 1989), which tells of the journeys of a Russian peasant in the nineteenth century, and of the prayer he learned and its impact on his life.

The prayer can be as short as two words, "Jesus...mercy." But its long form is "Lord Jesus Christ, Son of the Living God, have mercy on me, a sinner." The prayer is valued so highly because it uses the holy name of Jesus (e.g., Galatians 1:3) and the words of Scripture (see Luke 18:13, also 18:38); because it contains the heart of the gospel message of God's great mercy; and because its use can fulfill the biblical injunction to "pray without ceasing" (see Luke 18:1; 1 Thessalonians 5:17, Romans 12:12).

The prayer is used by being repeated. Under the guidance of a *staretz*, or spiritual director (which is sometimes still recommended as the way to learn it), the peasant began repeating the prayer a few times each day, gradually increasing until he was saying it several thousand times a day. What might happen eventually, as it did to him, is that the prayer "sinks" from the lips and the mind into the heart and becomes what is called "self-actualizing."

It is as though the prayer goes on praying, even without one being conscious of it; once in a while (as when one awakes in the morning or there is a pause in one's thinking during the day), a moment occurs and one realizes, "Oh, that's the Jesus Prayer." Thus, prayer without ceasing. This is a prayer one can use during personal prayer time, simply praying the words slowly in the manner of *lectio divina* as described above. One could also use the beads of a rosary to pray the prayer in sets of fifty.

One can use the prayer in other settings as well—for example, while walking—as a way of becoming accustomed to the prayer. Just match the rhythm of the stride with the rhythm of the phrases of the prayer. It can work like this. Left stride ("Lord"), right stride ("Jesus"), left ("Christ"), right (pause), left ("Son of the"), right ("Living"), left ("God"), right (pause), left ("have mercy on"), right ("me"), left ("a sinner"), right (pause); then repeat. With a little practice it becomes quite natural. Does it sound a little strange? Well, what *do* you do while walking? Why not pray?

As the *Catechism of the Catholic Church* says, "By a living transmission—Tradition—the Holy Spirit in the Church teaches the children of God to pray" (n. 2661). May these and the many other sources from our Tradition offer you and your students rich and varied guidance in the ways of prayer.

Your Thoughts

1 How do I discern and practice God's presence and movement in my life?

_____

_____

2 How did I learn to pray? What have I learned about praying?

_____

_____

_____

Try This

If you have not been on a retreat recently (or ever), make a resolution to participate in one in the coming year.

_____

_____

An INTRODUCTION *to* GREAT SPIRITUAL CLASSICS

FR. JOHN MCGRATH, SM

Catholic spiritual literacy means being familiar, informed, and transformed through our great treasury of Catholic literature.

T o live the life of Christ is the goal of the Christian. The Lord Jesus bestowed the gift of the Spirit on all believers so that they could live and grow in the life of Christ with the community of the faithful as the body of Christ. Those living a Christian life—fed by the Word of God in Scripture and the sacraments, especially the Eucharist—are on the journey of assimilating the salvific mission of Christ and bringing it to others.

This chapter considers how a few people—recognized by the church as remarkably helpful—responded to the call of the Spirit in and around themselves and left us some significant reflections, directions, and experiences that can guide and stimulate us in our days. They certainly are women and men of their times. But at the heart of their lives and work, their goal and longing are the same as ours: to live increasingly in relationship with Jesus Christ and share his mission for the sake of the flourishing of men and women in Christ.

St. Catherine of Siena (1347–1380)

Catherine lived and wrote at a difficult time in the history of the church. The popes lived in Avignon, not Rome, making life confusing for believers in a universal church. The black plague struck Europe in Catherine's childhood, and up to fifty percent of the population died. And the disease returned.

Catherine was the twenty-fourth of twenty-five children of a middle-class family. She was outgoing, pleasant, and independent. A "passion for the truth of things" was central to her as she matured. She worshiped often at the nearby church and cloister of St. Dominic. She was only seven years old when she vowed her virginity to God. At eighteen, she received the habit of the Dominican affiliates.

For a few years, Catherine lived a contemplative life. At twenty-one, she began her ministry of the Corporal Works of Mercy and spiritual conversations with people. Her prayer life involved mystical experiences and, in her many conversations, she learned the nuances of theology and Scripture from others while sharing with them her experience of the ways of God.

Catherine's social involvement led to interventions to promote peace among Italian cities like Florence, Pisa, Lucca, and Siena, plus reform of the clergy and the return of the pope to Rome. Called to Rome by Urban VI in the cause of unity and peace, Catherine carried on her ascetical community life as best she could, but her health gave way. She died in Rome at the age of thirty-three.

St. Catherine was a mystic. She led a highly active life, especially in her last twelve years, but she was led to this activity by her contemplation. Her classic work, *The Dialogue*, is the fruit of her prayer, much of it actual dictation during her prayer and from her own teaching and letters.

Catherine had no formal schooling, but she was completely orthodox in theology and in use of Scripture. Her influences were broad but especially Dominican, and she was at home with God's word. Her theology is not new. "What is original in Catherine is her capacity for fresh and vivid expression of the tradition," writes Suzanne Noffke, OP, in her Introduction to *The Dialogue* (Paulist Classics of Western Spirituality, 1988). Catherine's writings were not in Latin, as all the scholars' works were, but in her own Sienese dialect. This was another mark of the attraction of her writing.

St. Catherine's central teaching is Truth and Love. God is the "first gentle Truth," "mad with love" for us, and "charity itself." The way to God is the "constantly lived dynamic of knowledge and love."

Catherine was less a "social mystic" than a "mystic activist." In other words, her activism was driven by her prayer more than her prayer by her activism. Behind it all was her "tremendous desire for God's honor and the salvation of souls." She was declared a Doctor of the Church in 1970 by Pope Paul VI.

St. John of the Cross (1542–1591)

One of the great Spanish mystics of the Catholic Reformation, John was a leader of reform in his age, both respected and reviled. A saint (canonized in 1675 by Pope Benedict XIII) and a Doctor of the Church (declared in 1926 by Pope Pius XI), his reputation has seen a great resurgence of attraction in the last century as the contemplative movement has grown.

John was one of three sons born to a poor family. After a very basic education and during a job as a nurse and alms-seeker in a hospital, he took advantage of an opportunity to study Latin and rhetoric at a Jesuit school. These studies and other experiences with poetry and composition revealed and formed a very bright mind.

Joining the Carmelites, John was given the best education available in theology and philosophy in Salamanca. This brilliant student seemed headed toward ministry in education or theology, but the attractive austerity and contemplation made him think of joining the Carthusians.

Instead, he met St. Teresa of Ávila, and she persuaded him to become part of the Carmelite reform movement in which she was a leader.

Teresa and John emphasized mental prayer that they called *recollection*. "By the recollection...you withdraw from people and noisy places and enter within yourself, withdraw into the heart, unite the powers of the soul with the soul's highest part where the image of God is imprinted. Finally, then, prayer joins God and the soul, that is, 'the soul participates in the Lord himself and is perfectly recollected in him.'" This way of recollection had to involve one's whole life.

There was a great measure of success for the reforms, as Teresa and John founded Carmelite monasteries and convents in this new discalced or recollected direction. Progress, however, was far from smooth. The struggle for power among the king, pope, nuncio, bishops, visitators, and priors—as well as suspicions of Lutheranism—resulted in attacks, disavowals of support, imprisonments, exoneration, and sickness.

After some very hard times, most of John's last thirteen years were spent in positions of leadership. During this time, in Grenada, with an outstanding view of the Sierra Nevada and adjacent to the Alhambra, palace of the Muslim kings, John of the Cross wrote most of his poems and commentaries. He died in 1591 at the age of forty-nine.

Key to St. John's teaching is deification, the greater and greater union with God, which is the goal of human life. This happens through the elimination of everything incompatible with God and the gradual increase of God's gifts, graces, and virtues. The result is transformation.

John's work and significance slipped into obscurity until the end of the nineteenth century, when spiritual writers again grew to appreciate its richness.

St. Teresa of Ávila (1515–1582)

St. Teresa of Ávila is one of the great women of Christianity. Of the upper middle-class, Teresa was fifteen years old and one of ten children left behind when her mother died. Being outgoing and enthusiastic in personality, Teresa set out briefly at the age of seven, with her younger brother in tow, to be a martyr among the Muslims. Later, it was a struggle to get her father's permission and to maintain her health long enough to enter the convent at the age of twenty.

Mystical prayer, a strong sense of God's presence, and even ecstatic experiences were part of Teresa's early years in the convent. Although criticism of her prayer and explanations of her visions made her distrust herself, the advice of St. Francis Borgia and St. Peter Alcantara helped restore her confidence that her prayer was genuine.

Fellow Carmelites urged Teresa to take the lead in the reform of the Carmelite nuns toward a more prayerful and poor way of life, collaborating with the discalced (shoeless) reform among the men. Teresa accepted a leadership role. There were many reversals along the way for Teresa as provincials, nuncios, bishops, and kings, along with the religious themselves, sometimes supported and sometimes thwarted the reform movement. Her way was contemplative and active, idealistic and practical, rigorous and very human, and essentially feminine with some masculine traits. Teresa died at the age of sixty-seven in 1582. She was canonized in 1622 by Pope Gregory XV, and was declared a Doctor of the Church by Pope Paul VI in 1970.

St. Teresa's three major works were *The Book of My Life*, *The Way of Perfection*, and *The Interior Castle*. In *The Book of My Life*, the earliest of the books, Teresa describes the degrees of prayer by comparing them to a garden. In discursive meditation, using thoughts and reason, the soul is watering the garden by buckets carried from the well. In the next stage of recollection, this prayer is affective and the garden is fed by the steady prayer water wheel. In the prayer of quiet, a more passive stage, water rises from a spring or stream. In the last stage, union, God supplies the water—drenching rain.

In *The Interior Castle*, each room represents a different moment in the life of prayer, ranging from the beginning—when there is still a lot of reluctance about the spiritual life—to increasing openness to prayer, greater virtue, and closer union with God.

There are many books explaining Teresa and John of the Cross, and their ideas can sound very complicated. But as St. John says, all the faithful can have the fundamental confidence as "God himself is the one ultimate teacher of prayer who will most certainly provide all that is needful to those who humbly, patiently and generously place themselves unconditionally in his hands" (*The Living Flame of Love*: iii, 4b).

St. Francis de Sales (1567–1622)

The wounds of the Reformation were open and bloody in the time of Francis de Sales. A religious crisis seized the young devout Francis in the midst of an excellent Catholic humanist secondary education. Sick to despair about predestination, he accepted his radical dependency, abandoned himself to God's mercy, and was free to give himself to loving God to the fullest in the present.

Pursuing theology alongside his principal commitment to studying law, Francis was led to the conviction that God willed to save all people and that the divine name revealed on the cross was not "he who condemns" but "Savior." This conviction matched his experience of God's sustaining love and desire to redeem and a strong sense of human freedom to respond or not.

Francis decided to seek the priesthood and, as a priest of the strongly Protestant territory of Geneva, he sought to win back Geneva to Catholicism—not by battle but by personal reform and the power of love. As bishop, his great instrument for Catholicism would be an exemplary clergy, fervent monasteries, and bringing the gospel to the needs of all the community. He preached fervently, wrote, talked, and administered the sacraments.

Convinced that all women and men were called to authentic and fervent Christianity, Francis was also a spiritual director. For a woman at the French court who wanted to live her faith, Francis wrote many letters of direction aimed at realizing a greater love of God and living according to that love. These letters became the heart of his book *The Introduction to the Devout Life*, one of the most popular books of all time.

A more formal work of theological reflection and insight was the *Treatise on the Love of God*, a result of Francis' absorption of the entire wisdom of Christian history.

The spirituality of Francis de Sales continues to offer light for all who seek a life close and faithful to God. Our wounded but not corrupt human nature is oriented to God naturally. Each of us is graced to participate in our salvation and each is called to intimate communion with God. Abbess and stay-at-home mother, bishop and lay person, female executive and non-degreed rancher: all are called to realize his or her fullest capacity for the love of God. The one who seeks God doesn't have to go to the desert. An authentic life with God can be lived in the very busy world where we work and in our relationships with others.

St. Francis de Sales' "ask for nothing, refuse nothing" is a foundation for a holy kind of indifference and freedom in God's service. When Francis encouraged all to engrave the name of Jesus on their hearts, he meant that it is in the heart where the living Jesus comes to be. The heart is seat of both intellect and will. The spiritual life of a person, with the name of Jesus on his or her heart, is not primarily about understanding or enthusiasm but about the integration and engagement of the entire person.

In addition to *The Introduction to the Devout Life* and *Treatise on the Love of God*, two thousand letters of Francis have been published, although he probably wrote more than twenty thousand. He was canonized by Pope Alexander VII in 1665 and was declared a Doctor of the Church by Pope Pius IX in 1877.

24

Your Thoughts

1 St. Francis de Sales believed that an authentic life with God can be lived in the very busy world where we work and in our relationships with others. What is my experience of this?

_____

_____

2 What common factors do I observe in the lives of the spiritual heroes addressed in this chapter? Be specific.

_____

_____

_____

Try This

Read one of John of the Cross' poems and write a personal commentary on the poem, presenting how John of the Cross's spiritual perspective invites or challenges your spirituality.

SPIRITUALITY *and* POPULAR CULTURE

VINCENT MILLER

Any discussion of spirituality and popular culture requires a detailed consideration of the nature and function of popular culture. What is popular culture? How is it "popular"? How is it "culture"?

T his chapter considers the changing nature of the word "popular" as it has been used in theological and pastoral thought. It contrasts traditional popular culture and religion with the "commercial" popular culture with which we are primarily involved today. It then analyzes commercial popular culture from three perspectives: as a set of meanings, as a formation in cultural habits of engagement and use, and as a space that encourages certain kinds of interaction and discourages others.

Common Histories

Popular culture and popular religion share a common history. Both have long been viewed with suspicion by elite culture and clerical theology. Indeed, the pursuit of the spiritual life has been very much undertaken in contrast to the questionable faith of the mass of believers.

The religion practiced by most Christians in the history of Europe was an unruly blend of surviving paganism and magical understandings of Christian rituals. Against this, both Protestant and Catholic reformations were secretly allied—aiming for a deeper Christianization of Europe.

It was only after centuries of religious reform, modernization, and industrialization eroding peasant culture and traditions that elites began to romanticize popular culture as a bearer of what was being lost in modernity. In the French Jesuit scholar Michel de Certeau's words, popular culture could be revered as the "beauty of the dead" only after it had been politically defeated. Missionary practice conformed to this negative evaluation well into the twentieth century. Indigenous cultures and popular Christianity were viewed with suspicion.

Pope Paul VI broke with these assumptions. His 1967 encyclical, *On the Development of Peoples*, called attention to the loss of traditional cultures. His 1975 Apostolic Exhortation, *Evangelization in the Modern World*, called for the "evangelization of cultures" that would embrace and permeate particular cultures with the gospel, rather than being applied as a "thin veneer" that ignores the particularity of people's lives.

In 1979 the Latin American bishops at Puebla offered a positive evaluation of popular religion as a "storehouse of values that offers the answers of Christian wisdom to the great questions of life." Such an approach to popular culture has been developed extensively by North American Latino/Latina theology. Scholars such as Orlando Espin and Roberto Goizueta have argued that the religion of the people handed on through the generations in a rich network of beliefs, symbols, and rituals provides an important theological stream within the broader Catholic tradition.

This focus on the handing on of popular religion between generations—popular culture as a tradition—is a significant contrast with other uses of the term. In contemporary usage, "popular culture" signifies precisely what is not handed on in family and community. The mid-twentieth century saw the emergence of a youth culture marked by distinct music, cinema, dress, etc. Different generations now come of age with radically different cultural formations.

Such culture is still "popular" in contrast to the high cultures of classical music, literature, and drama. But it is no longer produced or handed on by the people themselves. It is produced, marketed, and distributed by professionals. For this reason, it is helpful to distinguish it as "commercial popular culture."

> One of the most fundamental challenges is encouraging a group to think about the contents of what it hears and views.

A Collection of Meanings

Even though "commercial popular culture" is produced by new forms of elites and distributed through commercial channels, it still functions somewhat like traditional popular culture. It provides a storehouse of symbols, attitudes, values, and narratives that form the backdrop of people's everyday lives.

The influential "Frankfurt social theorists" spoke of popular culture as "mass culture." The standard plot lines and predictable comic gags of mass-produced entertainment stripped culture of any critical edge, turning it into a tool to pacify the masses. Subsequent schools of cultural studies offered a much more nuanced read of commercial popular culture. Some is meaningful, uplifting, and challenging. Studies of how consumers understand and use popular culture find that audiences are often quite critical and creative.

A pastoral engagement with popular culture requires knowledge of its contents and attention to how it is interpreted and used. What types of music, television, films, and internet media are popular with a community? One of the most fundamental challenges is encouraging a group to think about the contents of what it hears and views.

The attraction to a given cultural object must also be classified. Some works are popular because they express something profound that people identify with—for good or ill. In that case, its meanings, symbols, and values can be engaged and critically correlated with the Christian message. Perhaps they are deeply compatible, and so the given work can be used as a dialogue partner or vehicle for discussing a Christian theme in the spiritual life.

The themes of love and fear running throughout the *Harry Potter* series are a case in point: the power of Harry's mother's sacrificial love; the fear that undergirds Voldemort's power and binds the Death Eaters together; Voldemort's fear of mortality vs. Dumbledore's and Harry's acceptance of it.

There are, of course, other works that present no such opportunities for correlation. Insofar as people are attracted to certain central themes, they must be alerted and challenged to the anti-Christian content. Celebrations of radical individualism are often wrapped in moving sentimentality or heroic bluster (e.g., *Out of Africa* by Isak Dinesen or *Atlas Shrugged* by Ayn Rand).

The *Harry Potter* series presents us with another line of analysis required when engaging popular culture. Whatever its deep themes, its storyline is cast in the myth of the special child—*Cinderella*, *The Ugly Duckling*, *The Princess Diaries*, *The Matrix*, etc. The underlying mythic structure may attract us more than the other content. Sometimes these other attractions should be engaged in themselves; sometimes they can be used as an entry into broader discussion of the content of a work.

Audience reception of a given film or song is quite complex. For example, JoEllen Shively studied Native American viewers of John Wayne's character in *The Searchers*. Although the film depicts the European conquest of Native Americans, many viewers identified with John Wayne's character—not for what he did in the film but for the quality of his character. His portrayal of a rugged, courageous outdoorsman resonated with their traditional values. Thus, a pastoral engagement with popular culture must take into consideration different attractions and be careful not to assume that viewers embrace the whole of a given work.

A Training in Habits

The very individuality of these engagements suggests the difference between commercial popular culture and traditional popular culture. Both are shared repertoires of images, songs, and stories, but contemporary popular culture is much more a matter of individual reception. We

29

encounter popular culture not through our families and neighbors but through commercial media.

Commercial popular culture treats culture as a commodity, and we often encounter commodities without knowing their origins. Of the myriad things we consume daily, for example, we know nothing of the hands that made them, the soil in which they were grown, the journeys they have made into our lives. It is not that we do not care; we do not know. The consumption of commodities trains our imaginations in shallow engagement. We are comfortable evaluating things with little knowledge of their full context.

Commercial popular culture brings these habits to the cultural realm. The popular song "Natural Blues" by Moby is a case in point. The dance song was built around a sample of the voice of Vera Hall recorded in her kitchen by Alan Lomax in 1959, singing the spiritual "Trouble So Hard." The song is a lament: "Oh Lordy, trouble so hard…nobody knows my troubles but God." Moby's song was enormously popular, featured in many soundtracks and commercials. Hall's voice brought a note of emotional authenticity, but listeners never learned of her story or of the religious and musical tradition out of which she sang.

Encountered momentarily within the broader media flow, culture is reduced to fragments of meaning that consumers piece together in their own contexts.

These habits influence attitudes toward religion. Just as we expect to be able to instantly understand a commodity or fragment of culture encountered in commercial popular culture, contemporary believers expect that religious traditions will give themselves to easy comprehension.

The commodification of religion looks a lot like the way of being religious that we find most comfortable these days: spirituality. We prefer to speak of spirituality rather than religion. We are suspicious of ties to communities and institutions. We are all expected to be seekers, developing our own religious visions as we pass through life, drawing elements from the many traditions we encounter. As we evaluate religious beliefs and practices, we hold on to what we find meaningful and leave behind what we do not. We focus on the individual's relationship to the Divine and are suspicious of any outside interference in this relationship.

There is a lot that is good about spirituality in this sense. It can generate greater individual responsibility for religious commitment, rather than passive belonging or relying on religious leaders. Spirituality emerges in a time when more laypeople than ever before are literate. They have access to more religious material than ever before—indeed the riches of all the great religious traditions.

> We embrace a hundred profound things but can't seem to change our lives. For that we need complex and shared beliefs and practices, community support, and challenge.

These positive aspects of spirituality come with serious costs. When we encounter religious culture in this way—removed from traditional and communal contexts—we lose two important things.

First, we lose the web of interconnections among religious beliefs and symbols that make up a religious tradition. These connections correct inadequate and extreme interpretations and weave doctrines and symbols into a holistic worldview. Commodified pieces of religious traditions are less likely to be complex, to make demands upon us that challenge us to live differently. They are ground down, like shiny, polished stones—more likely to conform to the preexisting shape of our lives than to challenge them.

Second, we lose the connections between beliefs and the practices, communities, and institutions that weave them into not just a worldview but a way of being and acting in the world. This seriously hinders our sincerely held, private spiritual beliefs and values from having a transformative effect upon our lives. We embrace a hundred profound things but can't seem to change our lives. For that we need complex and shared beliefs and practices, community support, and challenge.

A pastoral response should seek both to make the complexities of tradition accessible and to communicate that the fullness of a tradition is known only in a lifetime of reflection and practice. (This of course presumes a community in which such wisdom can be shared.) Traditional methods of interpretation should be taught as well, i.e., *lectio divina* and the Liturgy of the Hours as ways of reading Scripture, the particular postures and attitudes of liturgical prayer, etc.

A Place

Popular culture continues to change rapidly. The anxieties of previous generations about mass culture and passive consumption need to be revised in an age of popular cultural production. Blogs, Facebook, YouTube, Twitter, and other web-based means of sharing content make those with keyboards or video cameras their own producers. These new forms of popular culture hold great promise for the democratization of culture and global interconnection.

We must critically consider what these media forms allow. How much do they really allow us to share and communicate? In his 2011 World Communications Day message, Pope Benedict XVI cautioned: "In the search for sharing, for 'friends,' there is the challenge to be authentic and faithful, and not give in to the illusion of constructing an artificial public profile for oneself."

The new "space" of social media also raises the challenge of a culture that can float free of the physical space of bodies, society, and environment. As Benedict asks provocatively, "Who is my 'neighbor' in this new world?" Social media can broaden our connections beyond the confines of our local places. They can also substitute for them—enclosing us even deeper in comfortable worlds of our own choosing.

Conclusion

If the forms of popular culture have changed over the millennia, their challenge to the pastoral work of the church is constant because it is here that the gospel meets lived experience and culture. To turn away would be to fail the gospel and to write off culture.

What is needed is critical engagement that can question and challenge what is deficient and embrace and celebrate what is good.

Your Thoughts

1 Are there particular cultural traits that have been handed down through my family over the years? What impact do they have on my everyday life? My spiritual life? (Be specific.)

_____

_____

_____

2 What are the gifts and challenges of social media for nurturing my sense of spiritual communion within the faith community?

_____

_____

Try This

Reflect on the statement "The consumption of commodities trains our imaginations in shallow engagement." Test this reality in the lives of your family, friends, or students through guided conversation.

SPIRITUALITY *and* WORLD RELIGIONS

SR. JUDITH MARTIN, SSJ

Spirituality is a word that originates in a Christian context where it refers to a Spirit-guided reflecting on and living out of the gospel. Over the centuries, the term came to be used in the plural to designate different ways of living out the gospel mandate, as writers would allude to Benedictine, Franciscan, Dominican, Ignatian, and other spiritualities.

I t wasn't until the decades following the Second Vatican Council (1962-1965) that Christians in general and Catholics in particular began to recognize that other world religions had developed significant schools of spirituality. As a result, the term needed to be more broadly conceived in order to include expressions of Jewish, Muslim, Hindu, and Buddhist spiritualities, such as Hasidism, Sufism, Vedanta, and Zen, respectively.

Today, the internet and immigration have combined to make these and other forms of spirituality ever more accessible to individuals across the United States. Forty years ago, Protestant and Catholic churches, together with the occasional synagogue, defined the religious landscape of America.

Now, in the vicinity of a medium-sized city like Dayton, Ohio, one can attend a Dharma center to practice Zen meditation, a Tibetan center to receive guidance from a *rinpoche* (respected teacher), a Hindu temple to perform *puja* (worship) and practice yoga, and a *gurdwara* (Sikh house of worship) for chanting, as well as several Islamic centers for weekly worship and lectures on Sufi mystic poetry. Wherever we look we find confirmation of the fact that we live in one of the most religiously diverse nations in the world.

The comments that follow are designed to help religious educators respond to this new reality in several ways. First, it provides background information on how spirituality is understood and practiced in different faith traditions. Second, it explores the role that spirituality plays in contemporary interfaith encounters. Finally, it considers why we, as Christians, should encourage a critical openness to spirituality's many manifestations.

Many Faiths, Many Paths

A 25-volume series titled *World Spirituality: An Encyclopedic History of the Religious Quest* (New York: Crossroad Publishing Company, 1985-2003) attests to the fact that, although the word spirituality initially derived from Christian sources, it now has been adapted by the world religions. At the same time, a term well-rooted in many of these traditions can also be used to develop a working definition that accommodates the wide range of phenomena we will be considering.

Chinese religions call it *tao*, "the Way." Jews speak of religious norms as *halakah*, "the way to go." In Islam, guiding principles are known as *shari'ah*, "the path," and the classification of methods for its mystics, called *tariqa*, also means "the way." Hinduism, the oldest living religion, delineates three *margas* or "paths" to *moksha* (liberation), while Buddhists underscore an eightfold *marga* leading to Nirvana (enlightenment). Even early Christians were described as belonging to "the Way" (see Acts 9:2).

The brief survey that follows focuses on some of these paths but, in a way, only hints at the rich heritage of spiritual resources that have been preserved by the world's religions.

Hinduism We begin by looking at the oldest living religion: Hinduism. In this religious tradition, whose roots can be traced back at least five thousand years, Ultimate Reality is known as Brahman, "that which pervades all." Because Brahman is viewed as being beyond name and form, transpersonal rather than personal language is used. Thus, Brahman is commonly invoked as *Tat Ekam*, "That One." The goal is to be set free by becoming one with the One.

> The three paths are also referred to as jnana yoga, bhakti yoga, and karma yoga. Here the yoga means "spiritual discipline."

There are three classical ways to accomplish this. The more philosophically inclined are attracted to the "path or discipline of knowledge" (*jnana marga*). This path involves meditating on the One who is beyond name and form yet dwells within as our truest Self (*Atman*). It includes a practice of negating particulars in order to seek the greater whole. What Hindus refer to as *neti, neti*, "not this, not this," Christian mystics would call *via negativa* (the negative path).

For those more drawn to devotion, Hinduism developed the love-based spirituality of *bhakti marga*. Here the One reveals itself in personal forms as Krishna or Shiva or Kali to win over the devotee. As Krishna says in the *Bhagavad Gita* 9.29: "I am the same to all beings, and my love is ever the same; but those who worship me with devotion, they are in me and I am in them."

A third path is available for the "doers" like Mahatma Gandhi, whose tireless dedication to nonviolent action led to India's independence. This is *karma marga*, "the path of (selfless) action," where one serves without seeking a reward. From the viewpoint of a Hindu, Jesus qualifies as a *karma yogin* when he asks for the chalice to pass, but then selflessly surrenders his will (and his life) to God.

Buddhism Buddhists, by contrast, speak of Nirvana rather than God, yet they, too, have developed a number of spiritual practices. The goal is to free all beings from suffering, and the Eightfold Path provides practical steps for achieving this. Briefly stated, one is asked to live a moral life guided by compassion and aided by meditations that reveal the impermanent character of material things which, in turn, motivates one to live morally.

A practice developed in Mahayana Buddhism, now adopted by practitioners in different schools of Buddhism, involves taking the Vow of Compassion: a choice to forego one's own final liberation so that he or she can return to free others from suffering. Since the 1960s, this vow has been interpreted by the Vietnamese monk Thich Nhat Hanh as a call to bring mindfulness to bear on world issues. For Thich Nhat Hanh, this meant using the spiritual skills he learned in monastic training to develop peaceful ways of ending war. He called this "engaged" Buddhism.

Islam Islam has a number of practices designed to foster God-consciousness. One is to pray five times daily, fast during the month of Ramadan, and focus on God as the center of one's life as one circumambulates the *ka'ba* during the pilgrimage to Mecca (an experience which, it should be noted, led Malcolm X to rethink his anti-white rhetoric).

There is also the spiritual vision and practice of Islamic mystics, known as "Sufis." While most Muslims were content with the formulation "there is no God but God," Sufis went further. For them, nothing existed but Allah (God). Nor was it enough to submit to God; they wanted to *experience* God.

One way of doing this was by participating in a whirling dance in which they felt they were not only praying but also *becoming* prayer. In poetic language reminiscent of Christian mystics, they not only sought to see God and to see the world as God does, they also engaged in a *jihad* or (inner) struggle to remove all duality so that they could become the very eyes of God. Historically, it was their love-filled spirituality—and not any military *jihad*—that led inhabitants of Indonesia and Malaysia to adopt Islam.

Brief as they are, these thumbnail sketches reveal a spiritual trove, a legacy of wisdom for living that should not be ignored by other faith traditions.

Spirituality in Interfaith Encounters

Interfaith dialogue offers one avenue of access to the religious insights and practices of the world's religions. At first, the ecumenical movement nurtured by the Second Vatican Council led Catholics to associate dialogue with theological exchanges between members of different faiths. But a 1984 document titled "The Attitude of the Church toward Followers of Other Religions" can be credited with broadening the church's understanding of the term.

In addition to the dialogue of theological sharing mentioned above, the document (prepared by the Pontifical Council on Interreligious Dialogue) identifies three other types of dialogue. It speaks of a "dialogue of life," involving respectful interactions between people of different faiths in the course of daily life; a "dialogue of action," involving multi-faith collaboration on humanitarian projects; and a "dialogue of religious experience." The latter is the focus of attention here because it invites a mutual sharing of one's spiritual life and opens up the possibility of entering into religious practices identified with other faith traditions.

> A growing number of Catholics and other Christians find that interfaith sharing provides opportunities for deepening one's faith.

In some circles, participating in non-Christian practices is greeted with hesitancy and caution, mindful of Pope Benedict XVI's warning against relativism. There is a concern that this could lead to an attitude of indifferentism and a general weakening of one's faith.

Nevertheless, a growing number of Catholics and other Christians find that interfaith sharing provides opportunities for deepening one's faith. They look to the example of St. John Paul II and his willingness to cross religious boundaries to engage other faiths both theologically and in terms of social action and spirituality. They point to John Paul's decision, made just two years after the pontifical document had been released, to invite representatives of the world's religions to Assisi to pray for world peace. They watched also as this pope became the first pontiff in history to visit a synagogue and a mosque.

Dialogue of Spirituality

Why lay women and men across the Christian spectrum are attracted to the dialogue of spirituality is thoughtfully discussed in a concise book titled *Spirituality in Interfaith Dialogue* (Mahwah, NJ: Paulist Press, 1989). In this work, Catholic, Protestant, and Orthodox contributors reflect on the spiritual disciplines they have integrated from their lengthy encounters with Hindus, Buddhists, Muslims, Taoists, and others.

Here we learn from individuals who are neither neophytes nor dilettantes but committed Christians. We learn how their faith has been enriched by different forms of in-depth contact with other faith traditions: sometimes by reading the *Bhagavad Gita* side by side with the gospels; sometimes by joining in Buddhist meditation and centering prayer; sometimes by participating in Sufi dancing; or by attentively observing the painstaking creation and dissolution of a sand mandala. This, in turn, leads to interfaith sharing of beliefs and experiences, bringing forth new realizations and new commitments to working with others to build more just, peaceful, and loving communities.

For some, interreligious experiences lead to a sense of multiple belonging, or what theologian Peter Phan refers to as "being religious interreligiously" (*Being Religious Interreligiously: Asian Perspectives on Interfaith Dialogue*. Maryknoll, NY: Orbis Books, 2004). Perhaps the most prominent exemplar of this kind of openness is the recently deceased "dia-logian" (a theologian of interfaith dialogue) Raimon Panikkar. Born to a Spanish Catholic mother and an Indian Hindu father, Fr. Panikkar reflected on his own spiritual pilgrimage in this way: "I 'left' as a Christian, I 'found' myself a Hindu, and I 'return' a Buddhist without having ceased to be a Christian" (*The Intra-Religious Dialogue*. Mahwah, NJ: Paulist Press, 1999).

To outsiders, such talk may suggest identity confusion. Yet, the writings of mystics, East and West, attest to the fact that there comes a point in one's spiritual journey when an awareness of the Divine so expands one's consciousness that labels are transcended. Attaining a stage of what James Fowler calls "universalizing faith," certain individuals achieve a degree of spiritual liberation that is signified by either shedding all designations or by multiplying them.

> For some, interreligious experiences lead to a sense of multiple belonging, or what theologian Peter Phan refers to as "being religious interreligiously."

For example, we hear the Sufi mystic Shamsi Tabriz announce "I am neither Christian nor Jew nor Muslim," while Gandhi describes his religious affiliation by declaring "I am a Hindu, I am a Jew, I am a Christian, I am a Muslim." Perhaps this is the same kind of spiritual outlook that led Giuseppe Roncalli (St. John XXIII), the architect of the Second Vatican Council, to warmly welcome a delegation of Jews with the simple words "I am Joseph, your brother"—a gesture that in no small way marked a turning point in the history of Jewish-Christian relations.

Conclusion

In the twenty-first century, can we afford to ignore how the Spirit is present, as St. John Paul II said in his 1990 encyclical, *Mission of the Redeemer*, "not only in individuals, but also in…peoples, cultures, and religions" (n. 28)? Does not a healthy spirituality foster an openness to the truth wherever it is discerned?

Ignorance, hatred, and greed are embedded in our world and are the common enemies of all people of goodwill. Overcoming them requires cooperation, and this cannot occur unless schools, seminaries, and churches encourage understanding of other faith traditions in all their diversity and richness. As one eighth-century Hindu mystic said, "that religion is best that loses nothing of what is good in other religious traditions."

Your Thoughts

1 What has been my introduction to or experience of schools of spirituality other than Catholic?

_____

_____

_____

2 How many traditions exist within my community? How do these traditions mingle with the Catholic community?

_____

_____

_____

Try This

If possible, visit a worship center of a spiritual tradition other than Catholic. Read a book about another religious tradition. Share your insights with a friend.

SPIRITUAL HEROES *for the* TWENTY-FIRST CENTURY: MODERN-DAY SAINTS

MICHAEL J. DALEY

The gift and challenge of the saints lies not in any favors they may grant us but in the life of discipleship they invite us to experience.

S aints! They have long been offered by the church as our patrons and protectors, always ready to receive our petitions and prayers (not without a certain touch of superstition, mind you). Even more, their faith-filled lives have become for us images of God's incarnate image—Jesus the Christ. Ultimately, though, the gift and challenge of the saints lies not in any favors they may grant us but in the life of discipleship they invite us to experience.

Models of Holiness

In offering models of holiness, the church has long suffered from a public relations stereotype: saints are all male, all clergy or religious, and all virgins. Rather than make the call to holiness accessible, the canonization process appeared to present it as an obstacle removed from daily life and reserved for the elite few. The Second Vatican Council (1962-1965), however, stressed that the call to holiness is universal.

It is important to stress, then, that the church identifies Servants of God—Venerables, Blesseds, and Saints—not for their own benefit (they're dead when they receive the title) but for the sake of the living people of God. The lives of the saints show that holiness—authentic life in Christ—is possible in every age, occupation, part of the globe, and circumstance. In the process, we discover that, although there is only one holiness—God's—there are countless ways of living it.

Thomas Merton: The Incarnation Is Key

Thomas Merton (1915-1968) sought to flee the sin of the world. This led the Catholic convert to Kentucky and the Cistercian Abbey of Our Lady of Gethsemani in 1941. His journey of faith is described in the best-selling book *The Seven Storey Mountain* (New York: Mariner Books, 1999). For some years he immersed himself in the rhythms of monastic life, away from the temptations of the outside world.

Over time, however, Merton realized that the monastery is not a place set apart from the world but one intimately connected with it. He discovered that holiness has no boundaries as to where it is found or who has it. This belief was profoundly realized in an epiphany he had—not behind the monastic enclosure but on a sidewalk in the shopping district of Louisville, KY, at the corner of Fourth and Walnut.

Reflecting on the experience some years later, Merton wrote: "I was suddenly overwhelmed with the realization that I loved all those people, that they were mine and I theirs, that we could not be alien to one another even though we were total strangers. It was like waking from a dream of separateness, of spurious self-isolation in a special world, the world of renunciation and supposed holiness. The whole illusion of a separate holy existence is a dream."

As a result of this experience, Merton began to address topics like war and peace, racism, and other social justice concerns, while continuing to talk and write about prayer and spirituality. Merton showed us what we learn in Jesus' Incarnation—God entering into creation and becoming human. We are to embrace humanity with all its joys and sufferings.

Central to our own journey and struggle of holiness are these words of Merton's: "For me to be a saint means to be myself. Therefore, the problem of sanctity and salvation is in fact the problem of finding out who I am and of discovering my true self" (from *Seeds of Contemplation*, New York: New Directions Books, 1949).

St. Mother Teresa: The Light of Darkness

I know what you're thinking: "How can I compare with this woman—winner of the Nobel Peace Prize and visited by world leaders and celebrities?" Well, considering why these people came to visit her—the service she provided the poorest of the poor—we probably *can't* compare to her. But that's not why I offer St. Mother Teresa of Calcutta (1910-1997) as a model of holiness.

Where Mother Teresa may truly resonate with us is in our moments of spiritual doubt and darkness: "Does God really exist? Does what I do make a difference?" If we're honest with ourselves, perhaps these feelings are just as predominant, if not more so, than our attitudes of hope and assurance in the presence of God.

> Where Mother Teresa may truly resonate with us is in our moments of spiritual doubt and darkness: "Does God really exist? Does what I do make a difference?"

Few of us have known the anguish Mother Teresa experienced in her relationship with God. This was not short-lived but lasted the better part of her days. Writing to her spiritual director shortly before accepting the Nobel Prize in 1979, Mother Teresa said: "Jesus has a very special love for you. As for me, the silence and the emptiness is so great that I look and do not see, listen and do not hear" (to the Rev. Michael Van Der Peet, September 1979).

Commenting on this situation, spiritual writer Fr. James Martin, SJ, says, "Mother Teresa's work can seem far removed from our daily lives. Yet, in its relentless and even obsessive questioning, her life intersects with that of the modern atheist and agnostic. 'If I ever become a saint,' she wrote, 'I will surely be one of darkness'"(*New York Times*, August 29, 2007).

In a way, I see Mother Teresa's "dark night" as a parallel to St. Thérèse of Lisieux's (1873-1897) Little Way. Thérèse began and lived her religious life, fulfilling her duties—praying, cleaning, cooking, gardening, and doing laundry—to the best of her ability and with fervent love. Having undergone tremendous suffering over the years, Thérèse died of tuberculosis at the tender age of twenty-four in 1897. Little would be known of her were it not for the discovery and publication of her spiritual autobiography, *Story of a Soul*, in 1898.

In this small book, the world would soon discover Thérèse's way—the "little way" as she called it. "The Little Flower"—a name often attributed to her—communicates this idea well. Thérèse saw herself as Jesus' overlooked, forgotten, ordinary wildflower. This did not lead to despair, however, for she knew God was watching her do "little things with great love." Her little way was her path to holiness.

Maybe this is why Thérèse strikes such a chord with and appeals to so many people. Thérèse's life spent hidden behind cloister walls—like so many people's lives spent in the obscurity of fields, shops, and kitchens—proves that holiness is possible for everyone. In *Story of a Soul*, she wrote that Christ was most often present to her not "during my hours of prayer...but rather in the midst of my daily occupations."

St. John XXIII: Levity of Life

As seriously as they took their discipleship in Jesus, the saints had a lighter side as well—at least that is true of the ones I like best.

Take St. Lawrence, the fourth-century deacon martyred during a Roman persecution. In the midst of his torture on a gridiron, he is said to have cried out, "This side's done. Turn me over." He's not the patron saint of comedians, roasters, and butchers for nothing.

St. Teresa of Ávila, the sixteenth-century Carmelite reformer, wasn't above a quip of the tongue either. Thrown into the mud while riding a carriage, she said, "Lord, why did you let this happen to me?" To which God responded: "That's how I treat all my friends." St. Teresa quickly retorted, "Then it's no wonder you have so few of them." If God has a sense of humor, surely the members of his church must as well.

> Once, when asked how many people work in the Vatican, St. John XXIII replied, "About half."

This includes the pope. One of the funniest of all has to be St. John XXIII (1881-1963). Although he ushered in some of the most significant changes in the church through his convening of the Second Vatican Council, he had a lighter side. Once, when asked how many people work in the Vatican, he replied, "About half." Speaking of his peasant roots, St. John said, "There are three ways a man can be ruined: women, gambling, and farming. My father chose the most boring."

I believe that it was this sense of humor that allowed Pope John XXIII to look at the world with a sense of hope rather than despair. This was no more apparent than in his opening speech at the Second Vatican Council. Rather than take refuge in the negative readings of the state of the church and the world, Pope John encouraged a process of *aggiornamento* or "bringing up to date."

Pope John XXIII's words in the address that opened the Second Vatican Council still give us charge today: "In the daily exercise of our pastoral office, we sometimes have to listen, much to our regret, to voices of persons who, though burning with zeal, are not endowed with too much sense of discretion or measure. In these modern times they can see nothing but prevarication and ruin. They say that our era, in comparison with past eras, is getting worse....We feel that we must disagree with these prophets of gloom, who are always forecasting disaster, as though the end of the world were at hand."

It reminds me of the prayer that he is reputed to have said each night: "Lord, it's your church, I'm going to bed."

Although discipleship in Jesus is a serious matter, laughter has a grace like no other. I would argue that you can't be very holy without it.

Dorothy Day: God Wants Our Partial Successes

If there was ever a person who didn't want to be called a saint, that person was Dorothy Day (1897-1980). In fact, an oft-quoted line by her was, "Don't call me a saint. I don't want to be dismissed so easily."

Yet, with her Catholic Worker Movement companion Peter Maurin (and other contemporary figures like Cesar Chavez and Archbishop Oscar Romero), Day's work on behalf of the poor led people not only to take her seriously but also to see in her a holiness that we associate with the saints.

> Day was a lay woman whose life was somewhat unconventional. But holiness can be unconventional. It's not one size fits all.

Day was a lay woman whose life was somewhat unconventional. But holiness can be unconventional. It's not one size fits all. It's confusing, it's found in unexpected places, and it's lived out by people you'd never think able to meet the standards of holiness.

For Day, charity was never enough. Yes, she filled hungry stomachs and gave the homeless shelter. But just as importantly, she asked, "Why are these people hungry and unable to find shelter?" In the process, she questioned the very structures—economical, political, educational, sexual—upon which our society is based, and she found them wanting.

Day understood that charity is inseparable from social justice, and that personal morality has communal implications. This led her to create a newspaper and, later, houses of hospitality. Her manifesto was the Sermon on the Mount. In other words, she was trying to take the gospel seriously.

In response to people's comment that Jesus said, "The poor you will always have with you," Day would reply: "But we are not content that there should be so many of them. The class structure is of our making and by our consent, not God's, and we must do what we can to change it. We are urging revolutionary change." Yet, despite Day's best efforts, poverty, war, sexism, and materialism remain.

Conclusion

Where is the kingdom Jesus died to bring?

Here, I think is one of the great lessons of the saints: They are holy failures. Their dreams went unrealized. Yet, the former superior general of the Jesuits, Pedro Arrupe (1907-1991), said that it is as it should be: "The struggle for justice will never end. Our efforts will never be fully successful in this life. This does not mean that such efforts are worthless. God wants such partial successes. They are the first-fruits of the salvation wrought by Jesus. They are the signs of the coming of his Kingdom, the visible indications of its mysterious spreading among us" (address to the Tenth International Congress of Jesuit Alumni of Europe, July 31, 1973).

French novelist and essayist Léon Bloy once remarked that the greatest sadness in life was not to become a saint. St. Irenaeus said much the same thing centuries earlier when he stated that the glory of God was humanity fully alive. Our call to holiness—saintliness—lies in that very journey.

Your Thoughts

1 Who are some of my favorite saints? How do their lives inspire me? What is one particular characteristic of a saint that I want to model?

_____

_____

2 Why were Saint Teresa's moments of spiritual doubt and darkness an essential element of her spiritual journey and call to holiness? Does her experience resonate in my life? (Give an example.)

_____

_____

_____

Try This

Thomas Merton wrote: "For me to be a saint means to be myself. Therefore the problem of sanctity and salvation is in fact the problem of finding out who I am and of discovering my true self." Describe your spiritual journey toward holiness. Share your story with a friend

PATHWAYS *into* E-SPIRITUALITY

SR. ANGELA ANN ZUKOWSKI, MHSH

St. Bernard of Clairvaux wrote: "Everyone has to drink from his own well."

In this same spirit, Gustavo Gutierrez emphasizes that "spirituality is like living water that springs up in the very depths of the experience of faith." Thus, it is imperative for each of us to live our life "in the spirit of Jesus as you have encountered him in your concrete historical life" (*We Drink from Our Own Wells*, Maryknoll, NY: Orbis Books, 1985).

A variety of studies have been conducted and reported in Catholic journals and newspapers concerning Catholic inclinations and trends on spirituality and religion. Some reports indicate that the contemporary problems facing the Catholic Church are drawing Catholics away from the institutional dimension of the church (formal religion) toward an emphasis on spirituality (individual or selective expressions and rituals often separate from community).

A survey on American Catholics released in November 2011 addressed the question, "What does the emerging cultural tide of being 'spiritual but not religious' and believing in non-church-based forms of spirituality portend for the future of American Catholicism? Our study finds that while Catholics are imbibing the changing religious and spiritual environment, they also remain strongly wedded to the church's institutional tradition." (Research conducted by William V. D'Antonio, Mary Gautier, and Michelle Dillon. Highlights presented in the *National Catholic Reporter*, 10/28–11/10, 2011.)

The research goes on to say: "In sum, our findings suggest that while Catholics are embracing, and most likely will continue to embrace, new spiritual vocabularies and resources, it is also likely that they will continue to maintain a strong foothold in the church and to participate regularly in its sacraments."

Emerging Realities

This news may calm a catechist's concern and fear for the present moment. Yet there are emerging realities that catechists cannot ignore. These are associated with the evolving digital culture's influence on diverse e-spiritual experiences offered within the digital culture.

It is obvious from observing most young people that the digital-media culture is consuming a vast portion of their lives. Seldom is there a moment when some form of digital or social media is not connected to young people's hearing or vision—or both, as digital multitasking is the order of their days. Andrew J. Bacevich wrote: "Anyone who today works with or near young people cannot fail to see this: for members of the present generation, the smart phone has become an amulet. It is a sacred object to be held and caressed and constantly attended to" ("Selling Our Souls: Of Idolatry & iPhones." *Commonweal*, August 12, 2011).

Formal religion can become dazed and confused by the shifting tides or directions created by the digital culture that draws individuals toward online places and resources perceived to be more spiritually relevant. Nevertheless, let us have faith, for if God is alive and active in our world, then God will be creative in beckoning us toward a new transformation in catechesis to awaken the minds and hearts of our students in and through a digital age.

It is now essential that catechists seriously consider how to integrate the application of digital media resources and tools to reach our children every day or any time of the day. We want to communicate effectively the Good News with new spiritual imagination and immediacy so that our students can understand the call to discipleship in a digital age. Therefore, we need to overcome our resistance to the expanding digital culture.

"Linking" to Spirituality

Catholics have always benefited from an extensively rich treasury of spiritual practices for cultivating their spiritual lives. This book has identified many of these practices. Through the centuries, we have developed retreats, parish days of recollection, novenas, the Spiritual Exercises, pilgrimages, books, devotionals, and the richness of liturgical year celebrations, and these have served to enrich greatly our spirituality. Yet, changing lifestyles, limited time, and unreasonable distances make it difficult if not sometimes impossible to take advantage of the full wealth of these traditional spiritual experiences.

The digital culture can help. In fact, spirituality is one of the fastest growing themes being addressed within the digital culture. Type the word *spiritual* into a search engine and you, the cyber-catechist explorer, will discover a wide range of links to online resources, expressions, experiences, and interpretations defining the meaning of spirituality within diverse contexts. It is amazing to see how many links are there: spirituality (in general), 163,000,000 links; Christian spirituality, 5,040,000 links; Catholic spirituality, 2,160,000 links. Yet, the plethora of references can be confusing if you do not use a sound Catholic theological or liturgical grounding to interpret and evaluate these sites.

A participant in the University of Dayton catechist formation series e-mailed to comment and ask: "I heard in a workshop that e-spirituality is rapidly transforming young people's engagement with traditional spiritual exercises. Is this true? If so, what are catechists to do about it?"

This is a good question! While it is still too early to determine the radical influence e-spiritual experiences or movements may have on individuals and faith communities, we do know that we need to pay attention to what is happening in the digital world.

Digital Media for You

Faith formation can now be experienced anytime and anywhere via digital media. A growing number of faith-related online courses, seminars, and webinars are offered through Catholic colleges and universities around the country. Retreat centers, pastoral ministry centers, and religious communities are offering e-spiritual experiences for addressing the growing realization of the diversity faith needs within Catholic communities. For example:

- The Irish Jesuit website Sacred Space (sacredspace.ie) is an online version of the Ignatian Exercises. Without leaving one's office or home one can connect for up to ten minutes into a spiritual experience online.
- The Benedictine Sisters of Erie have created an online experience called Monasteries of the Heart, where individuals can meet other seekers who are looking for more meaningful spiritual-life experiences (monastereriesoftheheart.org).
- For regular online retreats, check out onlineministries.creighton.edu. Click on Collaborative Ministry and follow the links to online retreats.
- Visit the Henri Nouwen Society site for reflections on the spiritual writings of Nouwen (henrinouwen.org) or search online for Thomas Merton's writings.
- E-spiritual websites that catechists have found spiritually life-giving include prayingeachday.org, worldprayers.org, gratefulness.org, and beliefnet.com.
- Helpful sites in Spanish are rezandovoy.org, feadulta.com, and espaciosagrado.com.
- Among the most recent popular websites is bustedhalo.com, which strives to reveal the spiritual dimension of the lives of young adults through feature stories, reviews, interviews, audio

clips, etc. Also visit wordonfire.org. There you will find Fr. Robert Barron's blogs, video commentaries, chat rooms, articles, etc.

- On a more entertaining side, there is a creative blog called "Whispers in the Loggia" by Rocco Palmo (whispersintheloggia. blogspot.com). Palmo is a regular contributor to bustedhalo.com, with a biweekly column called "Almost Holy." Mike Hayes, author of *Googling God: The Religious Landscape of People in their 20s and 30s* (Mahwah, NJ: Paulist Press/BustedHalo Books; 2007), offers an interactive website with various e-spiritual opportunities for engaging young adults in their faith (googlinggod.com).

Digital Media for Your Faith Community

Parish websites are essential communication tools for offering e-spiritual links or opportunities to parishioners. Parishes are investing significant financial resources for designing attractive interactive parish websites that include e-mail, Facebook, Twitter, and blogs.

For example, parish online prayer rooms enable parishioners to request prayers and keep the parish informed of their spiritual or personal needs while nurturing the "communion" of the parish online. In fact, parishes are coming to realize that an integrated pastoral communication plan needs to be woven into the tapestry of the life of the parish.

Catechesis necessitates that digital natives—those who are skilled at utilizing digital tools and online resources—be available within the catechetical learning environment to support catechists. Therefore, the idea of creating digital parish ministries or a digital catechetical volunteer ministry, including young adults, is imperative today.

Digital Media for the Catechist

Why engage young adults in our digital catechetical ministry programs? This is their world! Here they are savvy and know how to navigate the digital terrain with comfort and ease.

Consider for a moment the young adults' use of mobile communications such as smart phones, which has created the so-called "texting" or "tweeting" generation. Texting or tweeting is an influence amplifier. Digital natives can assist catechists to extend their influence with their students in ways never before possible. Religious or spiritual thought—Christian messages, for example—is effortlessly introduced into this digital milieu. Some young people see texting as a way to share thoughts about God, spiritual experiences that awakened them to the presence of God, inspiring quotes, or experiences of the cross that call for healing and prayer.

Lori Erickson, a freelance writer, maintains The Holy Rover Blog at spiritualtravels.info. In "Seeding Cyberspace" (*America*, May 10, 2010), she wrote: "I started The Holy Rover, frankly, in larger part as a marketing tool for my work. During Advent last year I began to realize how much blogging was shaping my spiritual life. Each day I was forced to dig a little deeper into the meaning of the season, trying to find a new facet of Advent to write about." Erickson's comment is one frequently echoed by those who seriously engage in spiritual blogs for sharing faith, deepening faith formation, and creating online faith communities.

Lisa Hendey was looking for a way to prepare her sons to know more about their faith and prepare them for their First Holy Communion. She created a website that now features podcasts, videos, Facebook, and links to Twitter. Her website allows followers to exchange a wide range spiritual and religious information (CatholicMom.com).

The internet is blossoming into a new and vast Catholic library of online resources. Catholic publications are becoming online publications with alarming speed. Most Catholic textbook publishers offer valuable e-spiritual and lesson-planning resources. New interactive techniques for teaching and learning are emerging every nanosecond on educational websites demonstrating the application of digital tools and online resources. We are living in a fantastic, exciting new era!

Dream, Explore, Cultivate

We need to heed the words of Pope Benedict XVI in his 2009 World Communications Day Message: "It falls, in particular, to young people,

55

who have an almost spontaneous affinity for the new means of communication, to take on the responsibility for evangelization of this 'digital continent.'"

What does this mean for us as catechists or Catholic religion teachers? How do we measure the impact of navigating into this digital terrain (continent)—and the likelihood of success?

I believe that the likelihood of our success—as catechists applying digital resources for faith formation—lies in our abilities to enhance not only the spiritual life of our students but also the quality of community within our parishes. The attraction of e-spiritual experiences must be directed toward the integrated life of the faith community. For it is within community that we gather for the Eucharistic celebration, are nourished with the word of God, are strengthened with the Body and Blood of Jesus Christ, and know ourselves bonded as disciples for witnessing our belief amidst local neighborhoods and civic communities. High-tech and high-touch come together with a balanced digital faith perspective.

You may have come to this article with either vast or limited e-spiritual experiences. Your attitude or disposition for thinking about the application of e-spiritual resources into your lesson plans, homework assignments, or renewal experiences may vary. So it is prudent to be cautious.

Yet, the wonder of our present time is that there is a growing amount of online resources to support our catechetical ministry. The Catholic Church has only begun to dream, explore, and cultivate a vast landscape of e-spiritual opportunities to meet shifting lifestyles, diverse spiritual needs, and ongoing faith formation interests. Each one of us has a role to play in order to make use of the full potential this field has to offer our catechetical ministry. Therefore, our catechetical formation programs must introduce catechists to both the knowledge and the skills for navigating through the digital culture. Each of us needs the corrective lens of theological reflection and discernment to ensure that our choices authentically enable us to become effective digital catechists and catechetical leaders today.

Your Thoughts

1 Do the references to St. Bernard and Gustavo Gutierrez speak to my understanding of spirituality? How? Why? (Be specific.)

_____

_____

2 What has been my experience with the internet in searching for online resources on e-spirituality? What are my concerns with the results of my search?

_____

_____

Try This

Type the words _spirituality_, _Christian spirituality_, or _Catholic spirituality_ into a search engine and explore what is available. What new catechetical ideas emerge?

_____

_____

ABOUT THE CONTRIBUTORS

General Editor

Sr. Angela Ann Zukowski, MHSH, DMin, is the Director of the Institute for Pastoral Initiatives and Professor in the Department of Religious Studies of the University of Dayton. She is a member of the Mission Helpers of the Sacred Heart (Towson, MD).

Chapter 1

Fr. James Heft, SM, PhD, became the Alton Brooks Professor of Religion and President of the Institute for Advanced Catholic Studies (ifacs.com) at the University of Southern California in 2006. His most recent book, *Catholic High Schools: Facing the New Realities,* was published by Oxford University Press in 2011.

Chapter 2

William H. Johnston, PhD, is Associate Professor; Acting Committee Chair of Masters Programs in Theological Studies and Pastoral Ministry at the University of Dayton. He has held parish and archdiocesan catechetical positions, directed a diocesan ministry formation program, and chaired the board of NALM.

Chapter 3

Fr. John McGrath, SM, PhD, is a Marianist and has been a professor of Theology and Church History at the University of Dayton for more than 25 years. He has taught graduate studies in Switzerland, the Netherlands, and Canada, and has taught and preached retreats in India, Kenya, Zambia, and

Korea. A special interest is the Catholic Church in the twentieth and twenty-first centuries.

Chapter 4

Vincent Miller is the Gudorf Chair in Catholic Theology and Culture at the University of Dayton. He is the author of *Consuming Religion: Christian Faith and Practice in a Consumer Culture* (New York: Continuum, 2005).

Chapter 5

Sr. Judith Martin, SSJ, is Professor Emerita in the Religious Studies Department and former Director of the Women and Gender Studies Program at the University of Dayton. Martin teaches courses on world religions and feminist theology, has participated in interfaith activities in the East and Middle East as well as in the U.S., and has published a number of articles on women's spirituality.

Chapter 6

Michael J. Daley, MA, is a teacher at St. Xavier High School in Cincinnati, OH. His writings have appeared in a variety of journals including *Catholic Digest, America, U.S. Catholic, St. Anthony Messenger,* and *Momentum.* Daley's most recent work is *Reclaiming Catholicism: Treasures Old and New* (Maryknoll, NY: Orbis Books, 2010, ed. with Thomas Groome).

Chapter 7

Sr. Angela Ann Zukowski, MHSH, DMin (See General Editor.)

RECOMMENDED RESOURCES

**The following are available from the
United States Conference of Catholic Bishops
or your local Catholic bookstore**

National Directory for Catechesis
Washington, DC: United States Conference of Catholic Bishops, 2005

General Directory for Catechesis
Washington, DC: Congregation for the Clergy.
United States Conference of Catholic Bishops, 1997

New American Bible, Revised Edition (NABRE)
Washington, DC: United States Conference of Catholic
Bishops, 2011 (online at usccb.org/bible)

United States Catholic Catechism for Adults
Washington, DC: United States Conference of Catholic
Bishops, 2005 (online at usccb.org)

Catechism of the Catholic Church. Second Edition
Washington, DC: United States Conference of Catholic
Bishops, 1997 (online at usccb.org)

The following are available online at vatican.va

Constitution on the Sacred Liturgy (*Sacrosanctum Concilium*)
Second Vatican Council, 1963

Dogmatic Constitution on the Church (*Lumen Gentium*)
Second Vatican Council, 1964

Pastoral Constitution on the Church in the Modern World (*Gaudium et Spes*)
Second Vatican Council, 1965

On Evangelization in the Modern World (*Evangelii Nuntiandi*)
Exhortation of Pope Paul VI, 1975.

On the Development of Peoples (*Populorum Progressio*)
Encyclical of Pope Paul VI, 1967

Mission of the Redeemer (*Redemptoris Missio*)
Encyclical of St. John Paul II, 1990

Called to Be a Catechist

INSPIRATION AND PROFESSIONAL GROWTH

Now Available

The Role of the Catechist
9781627851558

The Vocation of the Catechist
9781627852876

Communicating the Faith
9781627852883

Breaking Open the Scriptures
9781627852890

Celebrating the Sacraments
9781627852920

Fostering Spirituality
9781627852906

Pondering the Parables
9781627852913

Coming in August 2018

Discovering Discipleship
9781627852937

Abiding in Prayer
9781627852944

Practicing the Beatitudes
9781627852951